MONSTER
CHRONICLES

Creatures from the Deep

STEPHEN KRENSKY

TEXAS ROSE

BOSTON

Lerner Publications Company · Minneapolis

Lerner Publications Company
A division of Lerner Publishing Group, Inc.
241 First Avenue North
Minneapolis, MN 55401 U.S.A.

Website address: www.lernerbooks.com

Library of Congress Cataloging-in-Publication Data

Krensky, Stephen.
    Creatures from the deep / by Stephen Krensky.
        p.   cm. — (Monster chronicles)
    Includes bibliographical references and index.
    ISBN-13: 978-0-8225-6761-5 (lib. bdg. : alk. paper)
      1. Sea monsters—Juvenile literature. 2. Animals, Mythical. I. Title.
    GR910.K74 2008
    001.944—dc22   2006030120

Manufactured in the United States of America
1 2 3 4 5 6 - JR - 13 12 11 10 09 08

TABLE OF CONTENTS

1

WHAT HIDES IN THE OCEAN?

The open sea is a dangerous place. Everyone knows that. But some dangers can still catch you by surprise. An Irishman named Brendan found that out firsthand. Brendan was an explorer who lived in the sixth century A.D. He was an experienced sailor. According to

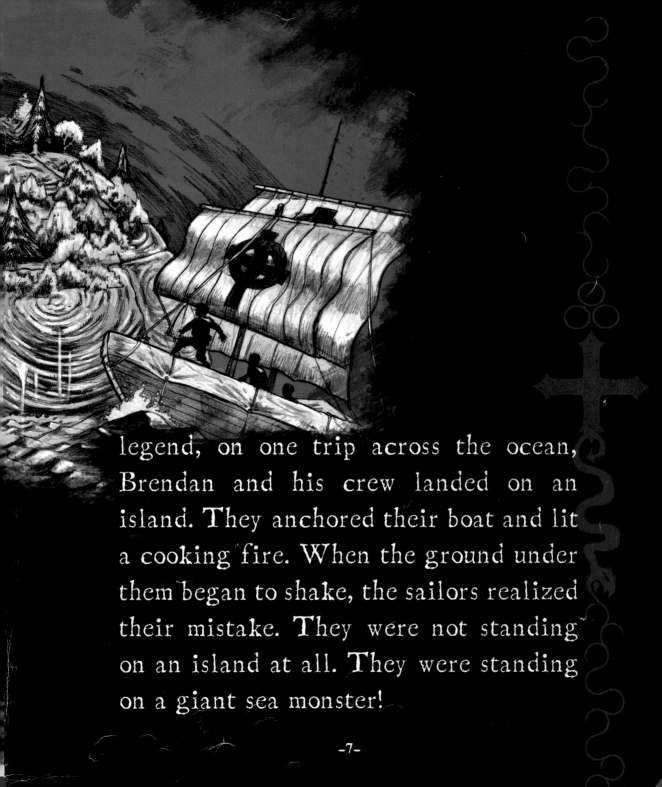

legend, on one trip across the ocean, Brendan and his crew landed on an island. They anchored their boat and lit a cooking fire. When the ground under them began to shake, the sailors realized their mistake. They were not standing on an island at all. They were standing on a giant sea monster!

BELOW THE SURFACE

The sea holds a lot of big creatures. Maybe that's because the sea itself is big. More than 70 percent of Earth's surface is covered in water. This water includes five oceans—the Atlantic, Pacific, Indian, Arctic, and Southern (or Antarctic)—and thousands of seas and lakes.

Near the shore, the ocean can be shallow. But there's plenty of deep water farther out. The average depth of the ocean is about 12,500 feet. Animals of all shapes and sizes live in this wet environment. From the smallest anchovies to the biggest whales, from starfish to seahorses, the sea is home to thousands of swimming, squirming, floating, diving animals.

Imagine ten Empire State Buildings standing one on top of the other. That's 12,500 feet—the average depth of the ocean.

Do sea monsters live in the ocean? Some people think so. Over the centuries, witnesses all over the world have reported seeing different kinds of sea monsters. Sailors on the ocean have claimed to have seen—and done battle with—sea monsters. People walking along the shore say they have seen them too. People have spotted sea monsters by day and by night, in every season, and in all kinds of weather. Reports come from ancient times all the way up to the twenty-first century. They come from China and the Pacific Ocean, the United States and the Atlantic Ocean, and all the places in between.

SOMETHING FISHY

Arabian Nights is a collection of Middle Eastern folktales from about A.D. 1500. In one story, the adventurer Sinbad *(above, from a 1930s British illustration)* lands his ship on an island. Then Sinbad discovers he's not on an island at all. Like the Irish sailor Brendan, Sinbad realizes he has landed on the back of a gigantic fish.

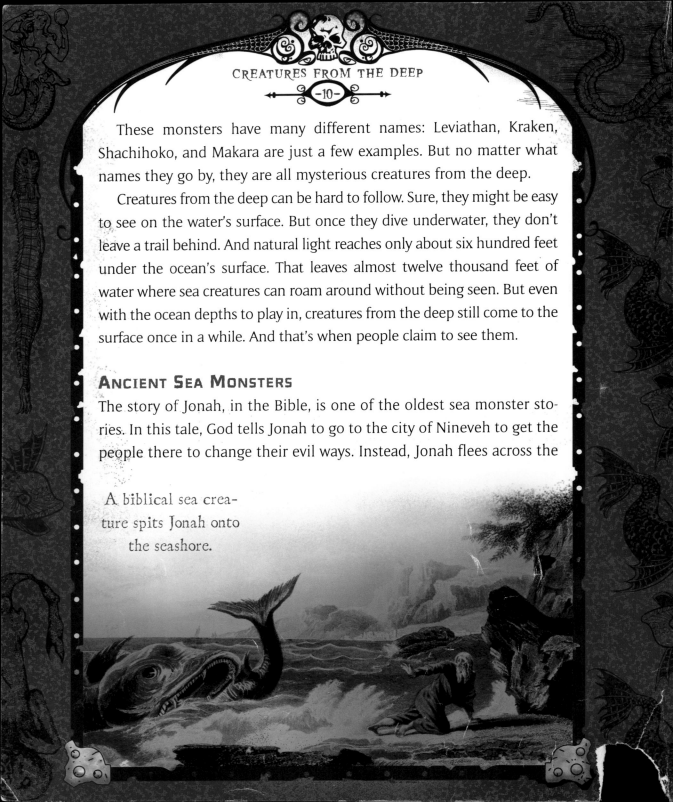

These monsters have many different names: Leviathan, Kraken, Shachihoko, and Makara are just a few examples. But no matter what names they go by, they are all mysterious creatures from the deep.

Creatures from the deep can be hard to follow. Sure, they might be easy to see on the water's surface. But once they dive underwater, they don't leave a trail behind. And natural light reaches only about six hundred feet under the ocean's surface. That leaves almost twelve thousand feet of water where sea creatures can roam around without being seen. But even with the ocean depths to play in, creatures from the deep still come to the surface once in a while. And that's when people claim to see them.

ANCIENT SEA MONSTERS

The story of Jonah, in the Bible, is one of the oldest sea monster stories. In this tale, God tells Jonah to go to the city of Nineveh to get the people there to change their evil ways. Instead, Jonah flees across the

A biblical sea creature spits Jonah onto the seashore.

sea by ship. When a storm threatens the ship, the sailors determine that Jonah is to blame. The sailors throw Jonah overboard, and a great sea creature swallows him. Three days later, the creature spits Jonah out onto the shore. In the King James Version of the Bible, first published in the 1600s, the sea creature that swallowed Jonah was called a whale. Whatever it was, the creature had to have been big enough to swallow a man whole.

The Bible tells of another enormous sea creature called Leviathan. The creature is not described in great detail, but there is little doubt about its enormous size. The Bible says that at first God created two Leviathans—a male and a female. Then God realized that if the Leviathans had children, they and their offspring would eventually eat everything in the sea. So God killed the female Leviathan, preventing the birth of any Leviathan children.

The ancient Greeks believed in many sea monsters. In Greek myth, two sea monsters, called Scylla and Charybdis, were particularly evil. Both Scylla and Charybdis began life as nymphs—beautiful women with special powers. But the gods changed them into monsters. In monster form, Scylla had six ugly heads, twelve dogs' legs, and a fish's tail. Scales covered her whole body. Scylla lived in a cave by the sea. She got her meals by snatching sailors from the decks of passing ships. Sailors made sure not to sail too close to Scylla. But in sailing around Scylla, they sometimes steered too close to Charybdis. She took the form of a whirlpool in the ocean and could swallow ships whole. (If she was not too hungry, she might pluck only a sailor or two as a snack.)

LUCKY HEROES

Jason, a hero of Greek legend, was among the few sailors to escape
both Scylla and Charybdis. Jason sailed on a ship called the *Argo*.
But even he needed the help of a goddess to make it past the two
monsters. Odysseus (*above*), another Greek mythic hero, also
encountered Scylla and Charybdis. Scylla devoured six sailors from
Odysseus's boat. Charybdis almost swallowed Odysseus himself. He
escaped her clutches by clinging to a tree at the edge of the water.

The biggest ancient sea creature comes from New Zealand. This island nation is in the South Pacific Ocean. The Maori people, New Zealand's first inhabitants, tell the story of a young man named Maui. Maui was a demigod, meaning that he was more powerful than an ordinary human but less powerful than a god. One day Maui went fishing with his two brothers. He dropped a magic fishhook into the water. After a while, he felt a strong tug on the line. But even with his special powers, he could not reel in the fish by himself. So he asked his brothers for help. Together, they pulled up a giant fish. It was as big as an island. According to Maori legend, Maui's fish was the North Island of New Zealand.

This Makara head is on a corner of the Jokhang Temple in Tibet.

In Scandinavia, people tell stories about the Kraken. This sea monster looks like a giant squid. It is large enough to crush whole ships in its tentacles. The Shachihoko is a mythical Chinese sea monster. It has a tiger's head, a fish's body, and poisonous stingers. Even scarier, the Shachihoko turns into a tiger when it reaches shore.

The Makara of India is an odd sea creature. It is a giant fish with the head of an elephant.

UNCHARTED WATERS

Olaus Magnus was a Swedish mapmaker from the 1500s. When
drawing maps, he included pictures of sea monsters swimming in the
oceans *(above)*. Magnus used the monsters to show that parts of the
oceans were unexplored and dangerous.

According to Indian legend, the sky god Varuna likes to ride on Makara's back.

Perhaps the most appealing creatures from the deep are mermaids. They are half woman, half fish. People from many different places and every ocean tell stories about mermaids. These mermaids are said to attract men with their beauty, their singing, and their golden hair. But sometimes, sailors trying to reach a mermaid will crash their ships into rocks. Some mermaids are mainly interested in luring sailors to their deaths. But others want real romance. Their male counterparts—half man, half fish—are called mermen.

FISH TALES

Most modern people don't believe in sea monsters. But in earlier eras, many people thought they were real.

Aristotle, an ancient Greek philosopher, thought that sea monsters were just ordinary animals—although they were rare and hard to find. (Aristotle thought unicorns and dragons were real animals too.) Explorers who sailed across the ocean were just as afraid of sea monsters as they were of running out of food or getting lost in a storm. Carolus Linnaeus, a scientist in the 1700s, came up with our system for organizing animals into groups and subgroups. He also investigated the Kraken and other sea monsters.

In legend, sea serpents swim through the water by moving their long bodies up and down, not side to side as snakes do.

According to early observers, sea monsters came in three basic varieties. One kind resembled a giant serpent, or snake. It was said to be hundreds of feet long and as thick around as a car. The second kind looked like a seagoing dinosaur. It had a long neck, a big body, a head like a horse or a lizard, and plenty of teeth. The third kind was a giant squid, with long arms, tentacles, giant eyes, and suckers. Some sea monsters had scales. Others had smooth, rubbery skin. Others were hairy. The creatures came in many shades of black, brown, and green—depending on whom you asked.

A Kraken attacks a ship. People have reported seeing Krakens for hundreds of years.

Eyewitnesses

In 1734 a Norwegian man named Hans Egede took a trip by sea. During the voyage, he saw "a very terrible sea monster which raised itself so high above the water that its head reached above our main-top [sail]. It had a long snout and blew like a whale, had broad, large flappers and the body was . . . covered with a hard skin." Egede added that the distance from the creature's tail to its head was as long as a ship.

In 1780 Captain George Little, a sailor from Maine, reported seeing a large serpent moving through the water at sunrise. Little's ship got within about one hundred feet of the serpent. He estimated that it was

forty-five to fifty feet long and about fifteen inches across. Its head was as big as a person's. The head rose several feet out of the water on a long neck. Almost forty years later, in the summer of 1817, two women spotted a similar sea serpent off the coast of Gloucester, Massachusetts. Over the next few weeks, other witnesses saw the serpent as well.

In the early 1800s, an Australian ship sat at anchor in an African port. In the middle of the night, according to a crew member, "something of a hairy nature" approached the ship. "By light of moon, its eyes could be seen large as a warrior's shield. It had tusks like those of a full-grown elephant." The ship's captain fired at the creature with muskets and pistols, driving it away.

MONSTERS ON LAND

Some people even encountered sea monsters onshore. Observers found one strange creature in Scotland in 1808. Fortunately for them, the creature was dead. "The body measured 55 feet in length," a witness wrote. "The thickest part might be equal to the girth of [a] pony. The head was not larger than that of a seal. It was furnished with two blow holes. On each side of the body were three large fins, shaped like paws."

But staying ashore did not ensure safety. Around 1820, a woman in Philadelphia, Pennsylvania, received a letter from her brother in Rhode Island. "Death, dear Elizabeth," he wrote, "has taken away your niece. The girl, while at the beach this summer a making of sand castles, was killed by a horrible monster what comes out of the sea. It had teeth, which it chewed upon her with. It had flappers like would be found upon a seal. Roared like a lion. Beat off four would-be rescuers."

During World War I (1914–1918), sailors sometimes fought in underwater vessels called submarines. One night in 1917, a mysterious beast was said to have climbed aboard a German submarine while the vessel sat on the water's surface. The creature had large eyes in a horny skull. The sailors attacked the creature. It returned to the water. But later, the captain found damage that he believed the monster had done to the sub. The craft could no longer dive into the water, and an enemy ship captured it.

Even in modern times, it seems that sea monsters still prowl the oceans. In 1973 Australian sailors found a monstrous creature draped over the front of their ship. It looked like a jellyfish, with long swinging tentacles. The sailors estimated that the creature weighed more than forty thousand pounds. They used high-pressure water hoses to blast the creature off the ship's deck.

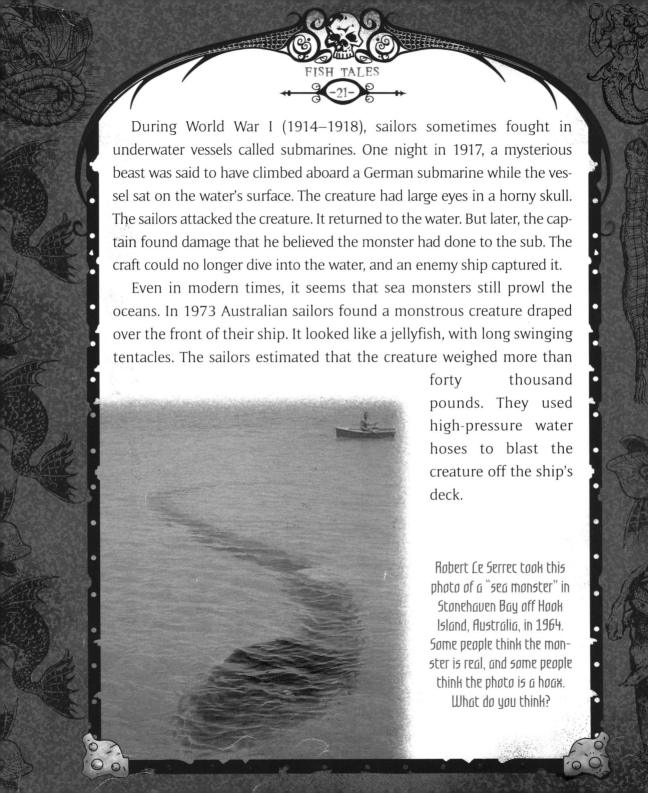

Robert Le Serrec took this photo of a "sea monster" in Stonehaven Bay off Hook Island, Australia, in 1964. Some people think the monster is real, and some people think the photo is a hoax. What do you think?

NESSIE, CHESSIE, AND CHAMP

Creatures from the deep don't live just in the open ocean. They also are said to inhabit lakes, bays, and other small bodies of water. The most famous of these legendary creatures are Nessie, Chessie, and Champ. Their names may be cute. But the creatures themselves are not.

Nessie, also known as the Loch Ness Monster, is the best-known lake monster. Nessie lives in Loch Ness, a lake in Scotland. The first reports of a monster in Loch Ness date to the sixth century A.D., when an Irish traveler saw a creature swimming in the lake. The reports picked up about two hundred years ago, and they have continued steadily ever since. In 1933 a vacationing couple saw an "enormous animal rolling and playing in the water." That same year, other people made similar sightings.

This snapshot of Nessie was taken in 1933 by Hugh Gray.

FOOLED YOU!

In 1934 a newspaper in Great Britain printed
a photograph of a creature *(above)* swimming in Loch Ness.
For sixty years, people wondered about the photo. Was it
really a picture of Nessie? Finally, in 1994, an old man
admitted that the picture was a hoax. He said that sixty years before, he and some friends had made a fake Nessie out of wood and a
toy submarine. They took "Nessie's"
picture and sold it to the newspaper.

In 1975 a priest saw a fast-moving, long-necked monster in the lake. Most witnesses agree that Nessie looks like a plesiosaur—a prehistoric reptile. Its head looks like a big lizard's head. The head sits on a long neck.

Since Loch Ness is very deep—one thousand feet at some points—it has plenty of space for Nessie to hide (and plenty of fish for Nessie to eat). In modern times, scientists with boats, sonar (a detection device using sound waves), and underwater cameras have explored the lake. They have tried to prove—or disprove—Nessie's existence. So far, no one has found Nessie. Skeptics, or disbelievers, say Nessie doesn't exist. Believers simply think that Nessie is just too smart to be found.

U.S. Monsters

Some monsters come from the United States. For example, Chessie (rhymes with Nessie) lives in Maryland, in the Chesapeake Bay. Observers say that Chessie is a long, thin sea serpent, between twenty-five and forty feet long.

Champ, another U.S. monster, is said to live in Lake Champlain, between Vermont and New York. The monster was first seen in the late 1800s, when it was known as the Lake Champlain Sea Serpent. Like Chessie, Champ is a serpentlike creature, with a head like a snake's. Most observers say it is twenty feet long. Lake Champlain is about 125 miles long, so Champ has plenty of room to stretch.

More than two hundred people are reported to have spotted Champ.

In the late 1800s, circus owner P. T. Barnum offered a fifty-thousand-dollar reward for proof of Champ's existence. Nobody was able to prove it to claim the reward.

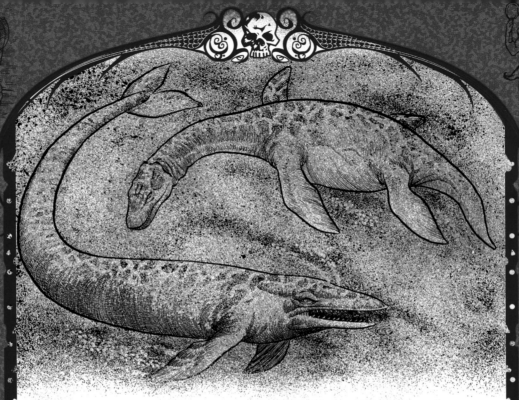

One was Sandra Mansi, who saw the monster in 1977. Mansi said Champ looked like an eel—but an eel that weighed two thousand pounds. She managed to take one picture before the creature vanished into the water.

No one knows for sure what Champ looks like. But artists have made a few guesses *(above)*.

At Port Henry, New York, residents have built a monument to Champ along the roadside. The monument is a sign that lists all the Champ sightings.

3 Real Sea Monsters?

Are sea monsters for real? Maybe not. But some real-life creatures from the deep are pretty unusual. Chances are, many sea monster stories are based on tales of these animals. For instance, seals and manatees look sort of half

human, half fish. They might be mistaken for mermaids. And kraken stories probably come from sightings of giant squids.

SWIMMING WITH THE DINOSAURS

Big animals are nothing new. Millions of years ago, some pretty big creatures were making a splash in the sea. One was the plesiosaur, which lived from about 200 million years ago until about 65 million

A plesiosaur *(right)* swims with an ichthyosaur.

years ago (around the same time as many dinosaurs). The plesiosaur had a small head, a long neck, and a big body with four fins. From head to tail, the plesiosaur could measure more than forty feet. It wasn't especially fierce. But it didn't have to be. It simply ate any smaller fish that swam its way.

The coelacanth appeared on Earth more than 300 million years ago. Modern scientists thought that coelacanths became extinct, or died out,

The megalodon was a prehistoric shark. It measured more than forty feet long—more than twice as big as a great white shark. Fortunately for everything that swims, the megalodon has been extinct for about one million years.

about 80 million years ago. The problem was, nobody bothered to tell the coelacanths. In 1938 fishers caught a living coelacanth off the coast of Africa. Scientists were shocked. Coelacanths weren't extinct after all. It wasn't like the coelacanths were trying to stay hidden. They were just swimming around, doing whatever it is coelacanths do. Coelacanths measure up to six feet long. They have large eyes and silvery blue or brownish gold scales. They have hinged jaws, which let their mouths open wide. The discovery of the coelacanth was exciting. But it also raised an interesting question: if coelacanths are still around, what other unknown creatures from the deep might be around too?

Museum workers in Kenya look at a coelacanth caught by Kenyan fishers in 2001.

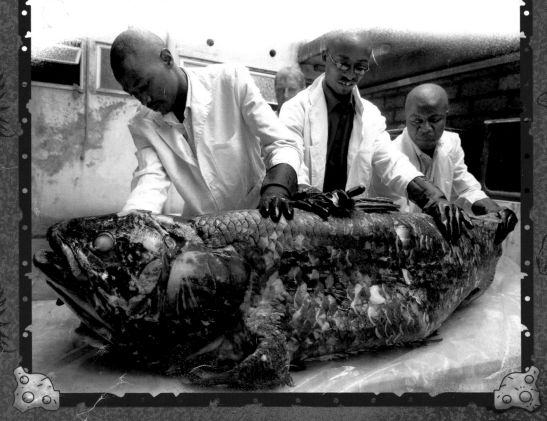

SWIMMING AMONG US

Except for the coelacanth, most ancient beasts are no longer swimming the seas. But plenty of modern sea creatures keep things interesting. The blue whale, for example, is the largest animal on Earth. At birth it can measure twenty-five feet long and weigh sixteen thousand pounds—about as big as three cars put together. And that's small compared to a grown-up blue whale. The longest blue whale ever found was about one hundred feet long. The heaviest weighed three hundred thousand pounds. Such big creatures can get pretty hungry. An adult blue whale can eat as much as sixteen thousand pounds of plankton (tiny sea creatures) every day.

The great white shark is another giant. It can grow more than twenty-one feet long and weigh more than five thousand pounds. It has a mouthful of sharp teeth—some of them almost three inches long. Great whites don't settle for plankton and other light snacks. They eat big fish. And if any people happen to cross their paths, great whites will eat them too.

A great white shark's teeth are serrated, like a saw blade, to cut and tear prey.

Big Fish, Small Portions

The biggest shark ever caught was a whale shark *(above)*. Fishers snared it near Miami, Florida, in 1912. It measured thirty-eight feet long and weighed more than thirty-six thousand pounds. (By comparison, a typical elephant weighs six thousand to ten thousand pounds.) Despite their great size, whale sharks have tiny throats. They eat mostly plankton.

Stories of sea serpents might come from the real-life anaconda. This water snake lives in South America. It can grow up to thirty feet long. All that length requires a lot of food, and anacondas are not shy about eating big meals. Mostly they eat birds and small mammals. If a meal is big enough, an anaconda may not eat again for weeks or even months.

For centuries, fishers told stories about giant squids. People already knew about ordinary squids—sea creatures with long bodies, eight arms, two tentacles, and round suckers on the arms and tentacles. But giant squids were said to be massive—up to sixty feet long and more

LONG AND SKINNY

The oarfish is sometimes mistaken for a sea serpent. It is thin like a ribbon. It can grow to be twenty-five feet long and several feet wide.

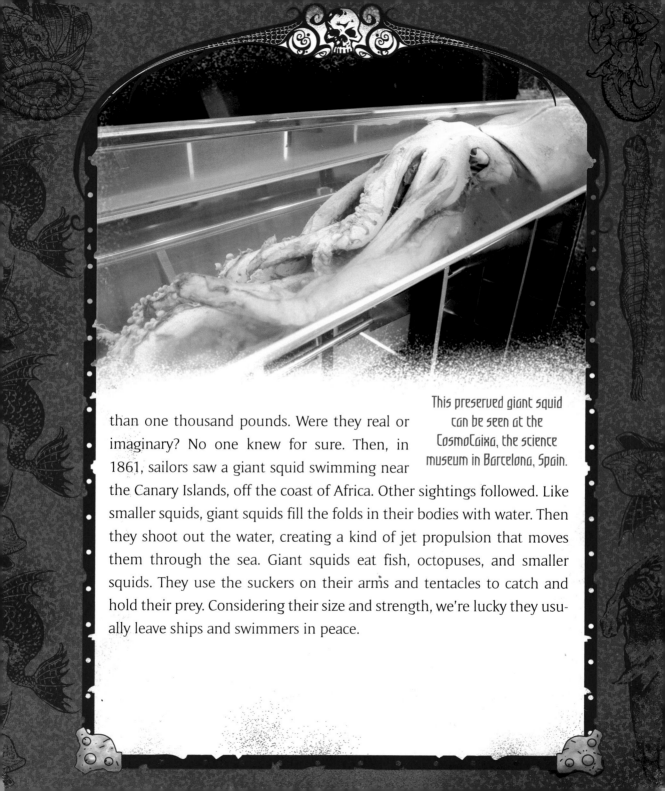

than one thousand pounds. Were they real or imaginary? No one knew for sure. Then, in 1861, sailors saw a giant squid swimming near the Canary Islands, off the coast of Africa. Other sightings followed. Like smaller squids, giant squids fill the folds in their bodies with water. Then they shoot out the water, creating a kind of jet propulsion that moves them through the sea. Giant squids eat fish, octopuses, and smaller squids. They use the suckers on their arms and tentacles to catch and hold their prey. Considering their size and strength, we're lucky they usually leave ships and swimmers in peace.

CREATURES THAT LIVE FOREVER

Not everyone is lucky (or unlucky) enough to see a sea monster. But all of us can read about them in books and even see them in movies. In that way, sea monsters will live forever. And we can all be eyewitnesses—even if the creatures we see are just creations of someone else's imagination.

A SEA OF WORDS

If you're curious about whale hunting, Herman Melville's book *Moby Dick* will tell you everything you want to know. And if you're interested in single-minded, peg-legged sea captains, this is also the book for you. *Moby Dick* was first published in 1851. It charts the course of Captain Ahab. He takes his ship, the *Pequod*, on a quest to find the white whale

Moby Dick has Captain Ahab in his grasp in this illustration from the 1850s.

Moby Dick. Moby Dick is famous among whales. But Ahab doesn't care about that. He does care that the last time he battled Moby Dick, the whale bit off his leg. Ahab thinks Moby Dick is evil and must be destroyed. What Moby Dick thinks remains a mystery.

Moby Dick, the whale in Herman Melville's novel, was a sperm whale. Sperm whales are the only big whales with teeth. Some of these teeth can be eight inches long.

Twenty Thousand Leagues under the Sea, by Jules Verne, is another seagoing adventure story. This book came out in 1870. It follows the quest of Captain Nemo. He explores the ocean depths in a fantastic submarine, the *Nautilus*. During the voyage, the *Nautilus* does battle with a giant squid—a monster that really does exist, even if Verne's *Nautilus* is made up.

Monsters and machines also figure in Daniel M. Pinkwater's *Yobgorgle: Mystery Monster of Lake Ontario*. This book from 1979 tells the story of a boy named Eugene. He goes on vacation to Lake Ontario with his Uncle Mel. Eugene meets Professor Ambrose McFain and learns about a mysterious lake creature called Yobgorgle. Is the monster real, or is it a hoax? Eugene and the professor are determined to get to the bottom of the mystery—even if their quest takes them to the bottom of Lake Ontario.

The Creature of Black Water Lake is a scary book from 1997. The author is Gary Paulsen. The book concerns young Ryan Swanner, who moves with his mother to Black Water Lake, a mountain resort. But this is no ordinary place of fun and frolic. The locals believe that an ancient creature lives beneath the lake's dark surface. Ryan doesn't believe the story at first. Neither does his new friend, Rita. Then Ryan sees some strange things around the lake. After that, he isn't sure what to believe anymore.

A SPLASH ON THE BIG SCREEN

Early on in the history of movies, filmmakers discovered that sea monsters make great movie stars. Both *Moby Dick* and *Twenty Thousand Leagues under the Sea* were made into movies. *Moby Dick* arrived on the

silver screen in 1930. *Twenty Thousand Leagues under the Sea* hit movie theaters in 1954.

The Adventures of Pinocchio is not a sea story, but it features a whale nonetheless. Carlo Collodi, an Italian writer, wrote the book in 1883. In 1940 the Walt Disney movie studio made an animated version of the story. Pinocchio is a puppet who wants to be a real boy. In the movie's most dramatic scene, Pinocchio is swallowed by a whale. Monstro is the whale's name, and it's an accurate one. Luckily, Pinocchio doesn't stay swallowed for long. He starts a fire inside Monstro. The smoke makes Monstro sneeze. Pinocchio rides that sneeze right out of the whale's mouth and back to dry land.

Filmmakers used stop-motion animation to create *The Beast from 20,000 Fathoms*. This 1953 film features real-life actors and one angry beast. The beast is a seagoing dinosaur. Millions of years ago, the tale goes, it was frozen in ice near the North Pole. A modern-day nuclear bomb test melts the ice. So the beast thaws out. There's not much to do at the North Pole, and the beast is eager to stretch its legs. So it heads south through the water. It ends up in New York City, crushing people and buildings with glee. Ordinary weapons don't bother the beast, so the army gets creative. Soldiers finally destroy the beast by shooting it with nuclear grenades.

Creature from the Black Lagoon put a scare into moviegoers in 1954. This film creature has gills and fins for living in water. But it also walks upright on two legs, which is handy for making trouble on land. In this case, the land is South America. Scientists who discover the creature won't leave it alone. They want to capture it—which the creature isn't very happy about. The scientists take the creature prisoner.

SPECIAL EFFECTS

Creature from the Black Lagoon (above) was originally shown in the 1950s in three dimensions, or 3-D. This technique made the action on the screen look deep, not flat. Moviegoers had to wear special glasses to see the 3-D effects. Had the creature been able to see the movie audience wearing their special glasses, it might never have come out of the lagoon.

It escapes and gets wounded. The movie ends as the creature retreats back into the depths of the Black Lagoon. *Creature from the Black Lagoon* was a big success, and the creature returned to star in two more movies.

Jaws was one of the biggest blockbusters in movie history. The 1975 film, directed by Steven Spielberg, takes place in a small New England beach town. Early in the movie, the peace along the beach is disturbed. A shark's fin slices through the water. The shark turns out to be a giant. After his first close-up look at the beast, the town sheriff says to his fellow shark hunters, "You're gonna need a bigger boat."

The 1975 movie *Jaws* made many people afraid of swimming in the ocean.

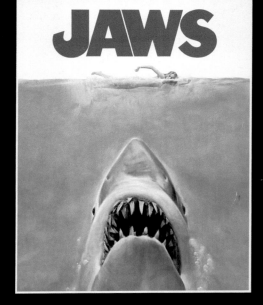

The terrifying motion picture from the terrifying No. 1 best seller.

JAWS

ROY SCHEIDER · ROBERT SHAW · RICHARD DREYFUSS

JAWS

Co-starring LORRAINE GARY · MURRAY HAMILTON · A ZANUCK/BROWN PRODUCTION
Screenplay by PETER BENCHLEY and CARL GOTTLIEB · Based on the novel by PETER BENCHLEY · Music by JOHN WILLIAM
Directed by STEVEN SPIELBERG · Produced by RICHARD D. ZANUCK and DAVID BROWN · A UNIVERSAL PICTURE
TECHNICOLOR® PANAVISION® **PG** PARENTAL GUIDANCE SUGGESTED ORIGINAL SOUNDTRACK AVAILABLE ON MCA RECORDS & TAPE
SOME MATERIAL MAY NOT BE SUITABLE FOR PRE-TEENAGERS ...MAY BE TOO INTENSE FOR YOUNGER CHIL

Warren Westridge, played by Jonathan Hyde, fights with a giant snake in *Anaconda*.

A bigger boat won't help much in *Anaconda* (1997). In this movie, a film crew in South America rescues a hunter whose boat is sinking. The hunter soon leads his rescuers on a quest to capture a giant anaconda. Since real anacondas grow to more than thirty feet, giant movie ones are quite a bit bigger. Not surprisingly, not all the cast members survive the encounter.

In *Lake Placid* (1999), something is nibbling on people along the shores of the lake. Well, *nibbling* isn't quite the right word, since the people being nibbled on disappear and are never heard from again. Rumor has it is that a giant crocodile is loose in the water. But how can that be? The lake is in Maine, more than one thousand miles north of any crocodile territory. The rumor seems ridiculous to the local game

A heart-pounding scene in the movie *Lake Placid* (1999) pits the local sheriff (played by Brendan Gleeson) against a huge crocodile.

warden and to a scientist called in to investigate. But they become believers as the mysterious creature claims more and more victims.

In the summer of 2003, famous filmmaker Werner Herzog set out to make a film about the Loch Ness Monster. He assembled a crew of experts, including a cryptozoologist—a scientist who studies legendary animals. But when the crew hit the water in Scotland, Nessie threw them more than a few surprises. Herzog's film, *Incident at Loch Ness* (2004), surprised and delighted audiences as well.

So far, we humans have been able to defeat most of the creatures that visit us from the deep. And the ones we can't defeat tend to wander off into the sea again, leaving us hoping they'll never come back. But you never know. Scientists believe that people have discovered only half of the plant and animal species on Earth. That leaves plenty of room for surprises.

-44-

SOURCE NOTES

19 Nigel Suckling, *The Book of Sea Monsters* (Woodstock, NY: Overlook Press, 1998), 7.

20 James B. Sweeney, *Sea Monsters: A Collection of Eyewitness Accounts* (New York: David McKay Company, 1977), 55.

20 Ibid., 54.

20 Ibid., 58.

22 Loren Coleman and Patrick Huyghe, *The Field Guide to Lake Monsters, Sea Serpents, and Other Mystery Denizens of the Deep* (New York: Jeremy P. Tarcher, 2003), 18.

SELECTED BIBLIOGRAPHY

Coleman, Loren, and Patrick Huyghe. *The Field Guide to Lake Monsters, Sea Serpents, and Other Mystery Denizens of the Deep.* New York: Jeremy P. Tarcher, 2003.

Ellis, Richard. *Monsters of the Sea.* Guilford, CT: Lyons Press, 1994.

Heuvelmans, Bernard. *In the Wake of Sea Serpents.* New York: Hill and Wang, 1968.

Soule, Gardner. *Mystery Monsters of the Deep.* New York: Franklin Watts, 1981.

Suckling, Nigel. *The Book of Sea Monsters.* Woodstock, NY: Overlook Press, 1998.

Sweeney, James B. *A Pictorial History of Sea Monsters and Other Dangerous Marine Life.* New York: Crown Publishers, 1972.

———. *Sea Monsters: A Collection of Eyewitness Accounts.* New York: David McKay Company, 1977.

Zarzynski, Joseph W. *Champ: Beyond the Legend.* Wilton, NY: M-Z Information, 1988.

FURTHER READING AND WEBSITES

Cryptozoology—Sea Creatures
   http:// www.floridasmart.com/subjects/ocean/animals_ocean_crypto.htm
   This website is an informative resource on all kinds of sea monsters and
   other creatures from the deep—both real and imagined, modern and ancient.

Dickinson, Peter. *Emma Tupper's Diary*. New York: Dell Yearling, 1988.
   When Emma Tupper arrives in Scotland to visit her cousins, she plans
   only to have a good time. But then she gets involved in a hoax to make an
   old submarine look like a real sea monster.

Herbst, Judith. *Monsters*. Minneapolis: Lerner Publications Company, 2005.
   This book discusses famous monsters and the stories that surround them.

Melville, Herman. *Moby Dick*. 1851. Reprint. New York: Bantam, 1981.
   This classic novel tells the story of Captain Ahab and Moby Dick.

Paulsen, Gary. *The Creature of Black Water Lake*. New York: Bantam
   Doubleday Dell, 1997.
   Ryan Swanner is not very excited about moving to the mountain resort at
   Black Water Lake. Then he learns that a large and ancient creature might
   live in the lake's dark waters. Naturally, Ryan wants to find out more.

Pinkwater, Daniel M. *Yobgorgle: Mystery Monster of Lake Ontario*. New
   York: Clarion Books, 1979.
   Eugene Winkleman goes on vacation near Lake Ontario with his Uncle
   Mel. He meets mysterious Professor Ambrose McFain and soon joins in
   the search for Yobgorgle, a monster said to live below the lake's surface.

Timeless Myths
   http://www.strangescience.net/stsea2.htm
   This site includes illustrations and descriptions of real and imagined sea
   monsters that worried sailors hundreds of years ago.

Walker, Sally M. *Fossil Fish Found Alive*. Minneapolis: Carolrhoda
   Books, 2002.
   This book relates the discovery of live coelacanths.

MOVIES

Anaconda, DVD. Directed by Luis LLosa. Culver City, CA: Sony Pictures, 1998.

    Computer-generated snakes never looked better—or bigger—than they do in this scary movie. A film crew in South America bites off more than it can chew when it runs afoul of a really big snake.

Jaws, thirtieth anniversary edition DVD. Directed by Steven Spielberg. Universal City, CA: Universal Studios, 2005.

    It's definitely not safe to go into the water in this 1975 classic. A great white shark decides that a New England beach is a good place to settle in for a few meals. When a team of shark hunters takes up the chase, they might end up on the menu.

Pirates of the Caribbean: Dead Man's Chest, DVD. Directed by Gore Verbinski. Burbank, CA: Walt Disney Video, 2007.

    This sequel to *Pirates of the Caribbean: Curse of the Black Pearl* again finds Captain Jack Sparrow in danger on the high seas. Among many other problems, a Kraken rises up to engulf Jack's ship at a crucial moment.

INDEX

ABOUT THE AUTHOR

Stephen Krensky is the author of many fiction and nonfiction books for children, including titles in the On My Own Folklore series and *Bigfoot*, *The Bogeyman*, *Dragons*, *Frankenstein*, *Ghosts*, *The Mummy*, *Vampires*, *Watchers in the Woods*, *Werewolves*, and *Zombies*. When he isn't hunched over his computer, he makes school visits and teaches writing workshops. In his free time, he enjoys playing tennis and softball and reading books by other people. Krensky lives in Massachusetts with his wife, Joan, and their family.

PHOTO ACKNOWLEDGMENTS